Simple 1-2-3™
KIDS

Publications International, Ltd.

Pictured on the front cover: Little Piggy Pie *(page 110).*
Pictured on the back cover *(top to bottom):* Cookie Sundae Cup *(page 119)* and Tuna Schooners *(page 67).*

ISBN-13: 978-1-60553-121-2
ISBN-10: 1-60553-121-9

Library of Congress Control Number: 2009933234

Manufactured in China.

8 7 6 5 4 3 2 1

Microwave Cooking: Microwave ovens vary in wattage. Use the cooking times as guidelines and check for doneness before adding more time.

Preparation/Cooking Times: Preparation times are based on the approximate amount of time required to assemble the recipe before cooking, baking, chilling or serving. These times include preparation steps such as measuring, chopping and mixing. The fact that some preparations and cooking can be done simultaneously is taken into account. Preparation of optional ingredients and serving suggestions is not included.

Publications International, Ltd.

Contents

Rise & Shine

Cinnamini Buns

2 tablespoons packed brown sugar
½ teaspoon ground cinnamon
1 can (8 ounces) refrigerated crescent roll dough
1 tablespoon butter, melted
½ cup powdered sugar
1 tablespoon milk

1. Preheat oven to 375°F. Generously grease baking sheet. Combine brown sugar and cinnamon in small bowl; mix well.

2. Unroll dough and separate into 2 (12×4-inch) rectangles; firmly press perforations to seal. Brush dough with butter; sprinkle with brown sugar mixture. Roll up each rectangle tightly, starting from long side; pinch edges to seal. Cut each roll into 12 (1-inch) slices with serrated knife. Place slices, cut sides up, about 1½ inches apart on prepared baking sheet.

3. Bake about 10 minutes or until golden brown. Remove to wire rack; cool completely. Blend powdered sugar and milk in small bowl until smooth; add additional milk, if necessary, to reach desired consistency. Drizzle glaze over cinnamon buns. *Makes 2 dozen mini buns*

Chocolate Chip Waffles

1 package DUNCAN HINES® Chocolate Chip Muffin Mix
¾ cup all-purpose flour
1 teaspoon baking powder
1¾ cups milk
2 eggs
5 tablespoons butter or margarine, melted
Confectioners' sugar (optional)
Fresh fruit, syrup, grated chocolate or whipped cream (optional)

1. Preheat and lightly grease waffle iron according to manufacturer's directions.

2. Combine muffin mix, flour and baking powder in large bowl. Add milk, eggs and melted butter. Stir until moistened, about 50 strokes. Pour batter onto center grids of preheated waffle iron. Bake according to manufacturer's directions until golden brown. Remove baked waffle carefully with fork. Repeat with remaining batter.

3. Dust lightly with confectioners' sugar, if desired. Top with fresh fruit, syrup, grated chocolate or whipped cream. *Makes 10 to 12 waffles*

Breakfast Pizza

    1 package (10 ounces) refrigerated biscuit dough
    ½ pound bacon slices
    2 tablespoons butter
    2 tablespoons all-purpose flour
    ¼ teaspoon salt
    ⅛ teaspoon black pepper
  1½ cups milk
    ½ cup (2 ounces) shredded Cheddar cheese
    ¼ cup sliced green onions
    ¼ cup chopped red bell pepper

1. Preheat oven to 350°F. Spray 13×9-inch baking dish with nonstick cooking spray. Separate biscuit dough; arrange on lightly floured surface. Roll into 14×10-inch rectangle. Place in prepared dish; pat edges up sides of dish. Bake 15 minutes. Remove from oven; set aside.

2. Meanwhile, place bacon in single layer in large skillet; cook over medium heat until crisp. Remove to paper towels; crumble.

3. Melt butter in medium saucepan over medium heat. Stir in flour, salt and black pepper until smooth. Gradually stir in milk; cook and stir until thickened. Add cheese; cook and stir until melted. Spread sauce evenly over baked crust. Arrange bacon, green onions and bell pepper over sauce. Bake 20 minutes or until crust is golden brown. Cut into wedges.

Makes 6 servings

Toll House® Mini Morsel Pancakes

2½ cups all-purpose flour
1 cup (6 ounces) NESTLÉ® TOLL HOUSE® Semi-Sweet
    Chocolate Mini Morsels
1 tablespoon baking powder
½ teaspoon salt
1¾ cups milk
2 large eggs
⅓ cup vegetable oil
⅓ cup packed brown sugar
Powdered sugar
Fresh sliced strawberries (optional)
Maple syrup

COMBINE flour, morsels, baking powder and salt in large bowl. Combine milk, eggs, vegetable oil and brown sugar in medium bowl; add to flour mixture. Stir just until moistened (batter may be lumpy).

HEAT griddle or skillet over medium heat; brush lightly with vegetable oil. Pour ¼ cup of batter onto hot griddle; cook until bubbles begin to burst. Turn; continue to cook for about 1 minute longer or until golden. Repeat with remaining batter.

SPRINKLE with powdered sugar; top with strawberries. Serve with maple syrup. *Makes about 18 pancakes*

Strawberry Muffins

1¼ cups all-purpose flour
2½ teaspoons baking powder
½ teaspoon salt
1 cup uncooked old-fashioned oats
½ cup sugar
1 cup milk
½ cup (1 stick) butter, melted
1 egg, beaten
1 teaspoon vanilla
1 cup chopped fresh strawberries

1. Preheat oven to 425°F. Grease bottoms only of 12 standard (2½-inch) muffin cups or line with paper baking cups; set aside.

2. Combine flour, baking powder and salt in large bowl. Stir in oats and sugar. Combine milk, butter, egg and vanilla in small bowl until well blended; stir into flour mixture just until moistened. Fold in strawberries. Spoon into prepared muffin cups, filling about two-thirds full.

3. Bake 15 to 18 minutes or until lightly browned and toothpick inserted into centers comes out clean. Remove from pan; cool on wire rack. Serve warm or cool completely. *Makes 12 muffins*

Triple Berry Breakfast Parfaits

2 cups vanilla yogurt
¼ teaspoon ground cinnamon
1 cup sliced strawberries
½ cup blueberries
½ cup raspberries
1 cup granola without raisins
Fresh mint leaves (optional)

1. Combine yogurt and cinnamon in small bowl.

2. Combine strawberries, blueberries and raspberries in medium bowl.

3. For each parfait, layer ¼ cup fruit mixture, 2 tablespoons granola and ¼ cup yogurt mixture in parfait glass. Repeat layers. Garnish with mint leaves.   *Makes 2 parfaits*

Quick Breakfast Sandwich

**2 turkey breakfast sausage
    patties**
3 eggs
   Salt and black pepper
2 teaspoons butter
2 slices Cheddar cheese
**2 whole wheat English muffins,
    split and toasted**

1. Cook sausage according to package directions; set aside and keep warm.

2. Beat eggs, salt and pepper in small bowl. Melt butter in small skillet over low heat. Pour eggs into skillet; cook and stir gently until just set.

3. Place cheese on bottom halves of English muffins; top with sausage, scrambled eggs and top halves of English muffins. Serve immediately.

Makes 2 sandwiches

Tip: Turkey sausage breakfast patties may vary in size. If patties are small, use two patties for each sandwich.

Banana Bread Waffles with Cinnamon Butter

½ cup unsalted whipped butter, softened
2 tablespoons powdered sugar
2 teaspoons grated orange peel
¼ teaspoon ground cinnamon
¼ teaspoon vanilla
1 package (7 ounces) banana muffin mix
⅔ cup buttermilk
1 egg
Nonstick cooking spray
Maple syrup (optional)

1. Preheat waffle iron. Combine butter, powdered sugar, orange peel, cinnamon and vanilla in small bowl; mix well. Set aside.

2. Combine muffin mix, buttermilk and egg in medium bowl; stir until just moistened.

3. Spray waffle iron with cooking spray. Spoon 1 cup batter onto waffle iron and cook according to manufacturer's directions. Repeat with remaining batter. Serve with Cinnamon Butter and syrup, if desired.

Makes 4 servings

Fudgey Peanut Butter Chip Muffins

½ **cup applesauce**
½ **cup quick-cooking rolled oats**
¼ **cup (½ stick) butter or margarine, softened**
½ **cup granulated sugar**
½ **cup packed light brown sugar**
 1 **egg**
½ **teaspoon vanilla extract**
¾ **cup all-purpose flour**
¼ **cup HERSHEY'S SPECIAL DARK® Cocoa or HERSHEY'S Cocoa**
½ **teaspoon baking soda**
¼ **teaspoon ground cinnamon (optional)**
 1 **cup REESE'S® Peanut Butter Chips**
    Powdered sugar (optional)

1. Heat oven to 350°F. Line muffin cups (2½ inches in diameter) with foil bake cups.

2. Stir together applesauce and oats in small bowl; set aside. Beat butter, granulated sugar, brown sugar, egg and vanilla in large bowl until well blended. Add applesauce mixture; blend well. Stir together flour, cocoa, baking soda and cinnamon, if desired. Add to butter mixture, blending well. Stir in peanut butter chips. Fill muffin cups ¾ full with batter.

3. Bake 22 to 26 minutes or until wooden pick inserted in centers comes out almost clean. Cool slightly in pan on wire rack. Sprinkle muffin tops with powdered sugar, if desired. Serve warm.   *Makes 12 to 15 muffins*

Fudgey Chocolate Chip Muffins: Omit peanut butter chips. Add 1 cup HERSHEY'S SPECIAL DARK Chocolate Chips or HERSHEY'S Semi-Sweet Chocolate Chips.

Bunny Pancakes with Strawberry Butter

Strawberry Butter (recipe follows)
2 cups buttermilk baking mix
1 cup milk
2 eggs
½ cup plain yogurt
Assorted candies

1. Prepare Strawberry Butter; set aside. Preheat electric skillet or griddle to 375°F.

2. Combine baking mix, milk, eggs and yogurt in medium bowl; mix well. Spoon scant ½ cup batter into skillet. With back of spoon, gently spread batter into 4-inch circle. Spoon about 2 tablespoons batter onto top edge of circle for head. Using back of spoon, spread batter from head to form bunny ears as shown in photo.

3. Cook until bubbles on surface begin to pop and top of pancake appears dry; turn pancake over. Cook 1 to 2 minutes. Decorate with candies as shown in photo. Repeat with remaining batter. Serve with Strawberry Butter. *Makes about 12 pancakes*

Reindeer Pancakes: Prepare batter as directed. Spoon scant ¼ cup batter into skillet. Quickly spread batter with back of spoon to form antlers as shown in photo. Cook as directed. Decorate as shown in photo.

Strawberry Butter

1 package (3 ounces) cream cheese, softened
½ cup (1 stick) butter, softened
⅓ cup powdered sugar
1½ cups fresh or thawed frozen strawberries

Place cream cheese and butter in food processor or blender; process until smooth. Add powdered sugar; process until blended. Add strawberries; process until finely chopped. *Makes about 1⅓ cups*

Sunny Day Breakfast Burritos

1 tablespoon butter
½ cup red or green bell pepper, chopped
2 green onions, sliced
6 eggs
2 tablespoons milk
¼ teaspoon salt
4 (7-inch) flour tortillas, warmed
½ cup (2 ounces) shredded colby jack or Mexican cheese blend
½ cup salsa

1. Melt butter in medium skillet over medium heat. Add bell pepper and green onions; cook and stir about 3 minutes or until tender.

2. Beat eggs, milk and salt in medium bowl. Add egg mixture to skillet; reduce heat to low. Cook and stir gently until eggs are just set. (Eggs should be soft with no liquid remaining.)

3. Spoon one fourth of egg mixture down center of each tortilla; top with 2 tablespoons cheese. Fold in sides of tortillas to enclose filling. Serve with salsa. *Makes 4 servings*

Tooty Fruitys

1 package (10 ounces) flaky biscuit dough
10 (1½-inch) fresh fruit pieces, such as apple, plum, peach or pear
1 egg white
1 teaspoon water
Powdered sugar (optional)

1. Preheat oven to 425°F. Spray baking sheets with nonstick cooking spray; set aside.

2. Separate biscuits. Roll biscuits on lightly floured surface with lightly floured rolling pin to form 3½-inch circles. Place 1 fruit piece in center of each circle. Bring 3 edges of dough up over fruit; pinch edges together to seal. Place on prepared baking sheets.

3. Beat egg white with water in small bowl; brush over dough. Bake 10 to 15 minutes or until golden brown. Remove to wire rack. Serve warm or at room temperature. Sprinkle with powdered sugar just before serving.

Makes 10 servings

Sweet Tooty Fruitys: Prepare dough circles as directed. Gently press both sides of dough circles into granulated or cinnamon-sugar to coat completely. Top with fruit and continue as directed, except do not brush with egg white mixture or sprinkle with powdered sugar.

Cheesy Tooty Fruitys: Prepare dough circles as directed. Top each circle with ½ teaspoon softened cream cheese in addition to the fruit. Continue as directed.

Strawberry Cinnamon French Toast

1 egg
¼ cup milk
½ teaspoon vanilla
4 (1-inch-thick) diagonally-cut slices French bread
1 tablespoon butter, softened
2 teaspoons sugar
¼ teaspoon ground cinnamon
1 cup sliced strawberries

1. Preheat oven to 450°F. Spray baking sheet with nonstick cooking spray; set aside.

2. Beat egg, milk and vanilla in shallow dish or pie plate. Lightly dip bread slices in egg mixture until completely coated. Place on prepared baking sheet. Bake 15 minutes or until golden brown, turning once.

3. Meanwhile, combine butter, sugar and cinnamon in small bowl; stir until well blended. Spread mixture evenly over French toast. Top with evenly with strawberries. *Makes 2 servings*

Prep Time: 10 minutes • Bake Time: 15 minutes

Snack Time

Maraschino-Lemonade Pops

   1 (10-ounce) jar maraschino cherries
   8 (3-ounce) paper cups
   1 (12-ounce) can frozen pink lemonade concentrate, partly thawed
   ¼ cup water
   8 popsicle sticks

1. Drain cherries, reserving juice. Place one whole cherry in each paper cup. Coarsely chop remaining cherries.

2. Add chopped cherries, lemonade concentrate, water and reserved juice to container of blender or food processor; blend until smooth.

3. Fill paper cups with equal amounts of cherry mixture. Freeze several hours or until very slushy. Place popsicle sticks in the center of each cup. Freeze 1 hour longer or until firm. To serve, peel off paper cups.

Makes 8 servings

Note: Serve immediately after peeling off paper cups—these pops melt very quickly.

Favorite recipe from **Cherry Marketing Institute**

Brontosaurus Bites

          4 cups air-popped popcorn
          2 cups mini-dinosaur grahams
          2 cups corn cereal squares
     1½ cups dried pineapple wedges
          1 package (6 ounces) dried fruit bits
             Butter-flavored cooking spray
          1 tablespoon plus 1½ teaspoons sugar
     1½ teaspoons ground cinnamon
       ½ teaspoon ground nutmeg
          1 cup yogurt-covered raisins

1. Preheat oven to 350°F. Combine popcorn, grahams, cereal, pineapple and fruit bits in large bowl; mix lightly. Transfer to ungreased 15×10-inch jelly-roll pan. Spray mixture generously with cooking spray.

2. Combine sugar, cinnamon and nutmeg in small bowl. Sprinkle half of sugar mixture over popcorn mixture; toss lightly to coat. Spray mixture again with additional cooking spray. Add remaining sugar mixture; mix lightly.

3. Bake snack mix 10 minutes, stirring after 5 minutes. Cool completely in pan on wire rack. Add raisins; mix lightly.   *Makes 12 servings*

Gorilla Grub: Substitute plain raisins for the yogurt-covered raisins and ¼ cup grated Parmesan cheese for the sugar, cinnamon and nutmeg.

Bananas & Cheesecake Dipping Sauce

½ **cup sour cream**
2 **ounces cream cheese**
2 **tablespoons plus 1 teaspoon milk**
2 **tablespoons sugar**
½ **teaspoon vanilla**
   Nutmeg (optional)
6 **medium bananas, unpeeled**

1. Place sour cream, cream cheese, milk, sugar and vanilla in blender; process until smooth.

2. Pour 2 tablespoons sauce into each of 6 small plastic containers; sprinkle with nutmeg, if desired. Cover tightly. Refrigerate until serving time.

3. To serve, partially peel banana and dip directly into sauce; continue to peel and dip. *Makes 6 servings*

Tropical Coconut Cream Dipping Sauce: Substitute coconut extract for vanilla.

Pizza Turnovers

   5 ounces mild Italian turkey sausage
   ½ cup prepared pizza sauce
   1 package (10 ounces) refrigerated pizza dough
   ⅓ cup shredded Italian cheese blend

1. Preheat oven to 425°F. Spray baking sheet with olive oil cooking spray. Brown sausage in nonstick saucepan, stirring to break up meat. Drain fat. Add pizza sauce; cook and stir until heated through.

2. Unroll pizza dough; pat into 12×8-inch rectangle. Cut into 6 (4×4-inch) squares. Divide sausage mixture evenly among squares; sprinkle with cheese. Lift one corner of each square; fold over filling to opposite corner to form triangle. Press edges with tines of fork to seal. Place on prepared baking sheet.

3. Bake 11 to 13 minutes or until golden brown. Serve immediately.

Makes 6 servings

Note: To freeze turnovers, remove to wire rack to cool 30 minutes. Wrap individually in plastic wrap; place in large resealable food storage bag and freeze. To reheat turnovers, preheat oven to 400°F. Unwrap turnovers; place on ungreased baking sheet. Cover loosely with foil. Bake 18 to 22 minutes or until heated through. Or place one turnover on a paper towel-lined microwavable plate. Microwave on LOW (30%) 3 to 3½ minutes or until heated through, turning once.

Green Meanies

4 green apples
1 cup peanut butter
Slivered almonds

1. Place apple, stem side up, on cutting board. Cut away 2 halves from sides of apple, leaving 1-inch-thick center slice with stem and core. Discard core slice. Cut each half in half. Then cut each apple quarter into two wedges using a crinkle cutter. Each apple will yield 8 wedges.

2. Spread 2 teaspoons peanut butter on wide edge of apple slice. Top with another crinkled edge apple slice, aligning crinkled edges to resemble jaws.

3. Insert almond slivers to make fangs.   *Makes 8 servings*

Tip: To keep the apples slices from turning brown, dip them in lemon juice before spreading with peanut butter.

HERSHEY'S Easy Chocolate Cracker Snacks

1⅔ cups (10-ounce package) HERSHEY'S Mint Chocolate Chips*
**2 cups (12-ounce package) HERSHEY'S SPECIAL DARK® Chocolate Chips
    or HERSHEY'S Semi-Sweet Chocolate Chips**
2 tablespoons shortening (do not use butter, margarine, spread or oil)
60 to 70 round buttery crackers (about one-half 1-pound box)

*2 cups (11.5-ounce package) HERSHEY'S Milk Chocolate Chips and ¼ teaspoon pure peppermint extract can be substituted for mint chocolate chips.

1. Line several trays or cookie sheets with wax paper.

2. Place mint chocolate chips, chocolate chips and shortening in large microwave-safe bowl. Microwave at MEDIUM (50%) 1 minute; stir. Continue heating 30 seconds at a time, stirring after each heating, until chips are melted and mixture is smooth when stirred.

3. Drop crackers into chocolate mixture one at a time. Using tongs, push cracker into chocolate so that it is covered completely. (If chocolate begins to thicken, reheat 10 to 20 seconds in microwave.) Remove from chocolate, tapping lightly on edge of bowl to remove excess chocolate. Place on prepared tray. Refrigerate until chocolate hardens, about 20 minutes. For best results, store tightly covered in refrigerator.

Makes about 5½ dozen crackers

Peanut Butter and Milk Chocolate: Use 1⅔ cups (10-ounce package) REESE'S® Peanut Butter Chips, 2 cups (11.5-ounce package) HERSHEY'S Milk Chocolate Chips and 2 tablespoons shortening. Proceed as directed.

White Chip and Toffee: Melt 2 bags (12 ounces each) HERSHEY'S Premier White Chips and 2 tablespoons shortening. Dip crackers; before coating hardens, sprinkle with HEATH® BITS 'O BRICKLE® Toffee Bits.

Bread Pudding Snacks

1¼ cups milk
½ cup cholesterol-free egg substitute
⅓ cup sugar
1 teaspoon vanilla
⅛ teaspoon salt
⅛ teaspoon ground nutmeg (optional)
4 cups ½-inch cinnamon or cinnamon-raisin bread cubes
    (about 6 bread slices)
1 tablespoon butter, melted

1. Combine milk, egg substitute, sugar, vanilla, salt and nutmeg, if desired, in medium bowl; mix well. Add bread; mix until well moistened. Let stand at room temperature 15 minutes.

2. Preheat oven to 350°F. Line 12 standard (2½-inch) muffin cups with paper baking cups. Spoon bread mixture evenly into prepared cups; drizzle evenly with butter.

3. Bake 30 to 35 minutes or until snacks are puffed and golden brown. Remove to wire rack; cool completely.   *Makes 12 servings*

Note: Snacks will puff up in the oven and fall slightly upon cooling.

Señor Nacho Dip

½ **package (4 ounces) cream cheese, cubed**
½ **cup (2 ounces) shredded Cheddar cheese**
¼ **cup mild or medium chunky salsa**
 2 **teaspoons milk**
 4 **ounces baked tortilla chips or assorted fresh vegetable dippers**
  Hot chile peppers (optional)
  Chopped cilantro (optional)

1. Combine cream cheese and Cheddar cheese in small saucepan; cook and stir over low heat until melted.

2. Stir in salsa and milk; cook and stir until heated through.

3. Transfer dip to small serving bowl. Serve with tortilla chips. Garnish with hot peppers and cilantro.   *Makes 4 servings*

Olé Dip: Substitute Monterey Jack cheese or taco cheese for Cheddar cheese.

Spicy Mustard Dip: Omit tortilla chips. Substitute 2 teaspoons spicy brown mustard or honey mustard for salsa. Serve with fresh vegetable dippers or pretzels.

Peanut Butter & Jelly Shakes

1½ cups vanilla ice cream
¼ cup milk
2 tablespoons creamy peanut butter
6 peanut butter sandwich cookies, coarsely chopped
¼ cup strawberry jam

1. Place ice cream, milk and peanut butter in blender. Process 1 to 2 minutes or until smooth.

2. Add chopped cookies; blend 10 seconds at low speed. Pour into 2 glasses.

3. Place jam and 1 to 2 teaspoons water in small bowl; stir until smooth. Stir 2 tablespoons jam mixture into each glass. Serve immediately.

Makes 2 servings

Variation: Use any flavor of jam in place of strawberry.

Prep Time: 10 minutes

Quick S'More

1 whole graham cracker
1 large marshmallow
1 teaspoon hot fudge topping

1. Break graham cracker in half crosswise. Place one half on microwavable plate; top with marshmallow.

2. Spread remaining half of cracker with hot fudge topping.

3. Place cracker with marshmallow in microwave. Microwave on HIGH 12 to 14 seconds or until marshmallow puffs up. Immediately place remaining cracker, fudge side down, over marshmallow. Press crackers gently to even out marshmallow layer. Cool slightly. *Makes 1 serving*

Tip: Cooled S'mores can be made the night before and wrapped in plastic wrap or sealed in a small resealable food storage bag. Store at room temperature until ready to serve.

Honey Crunch Popcorn

12 cups air-popped popcorn
½ cup chopped pecans
½ cup packed brown sugar
½ cup honey

1. Preheat oven to 300°F. Spray baking sheet with nonstick cooking spray; set aside.

2. Combine popcorn and pecans in large bowl; mix lightly. Set aside. Combine brown sugar and honey in small saucepan; cook and stir over medium heat just until brown sugar is dissolved and mixture comes to a boil. Pour over popcorn mixture; toss lightly to coat. Transfer to prepared baking sheet.

3. Bake 30 minutes, stirring after 15 minutes. Spray large sheet of waxed paper with cooking spray. Transfer popcorn to prepared waxed paper to cool. Store in airtight containers. *Makes 12 servings*

Variation: Add 1 cup chopped, mixed dried fruit immediately after removing popcorn from oven.

Fantasy Cinnamon Applewiches

4 slices raisin bread
⅓ cup cream cheese, softened
¼ cup finely chopped unpeeled apple
1 teaspoon sugar
⅛ teaspoon ground cinnamon

1. Toast bread. Cut into desired shapes using large cookie cutters.

2. Combine cream cheese and apple in small bowl; spread onto toast.

3. Combine sugar and cinnamon in another small bowl; sprinkle evenly over cream cheese mixture.   *Makes 4 servings*

Tip: Create your own fun shapes, but be sure to have an adult cut out your requested shape with a serrated knife for best results.

Peanut Pitas

4 small (4-inch) rounds pita bread, cut in half
16 teaspoons peanut butter
16 teaspoons strawberry fruit spread
1 large banana, peeled and thinly sliced (about 48 slices)

1. Spread inside of each pita half with 1 teaspoon peanut butter and 1 teaspoon fruit spread.

2. Fill pita halves evenly with banana slices. Serve immediately.

Makes 8 servings

Honey Bees: Substitute honey for fruit spread.

Jolly Jellies: Substitute any flavor jelly for fruit spread and thin apple slices for banana slices.

P.B. Crunchers: Substitute mayonnaise for fruit spread and celery slices for banana slices.

Swimming Tuna Dip

1 cup cottage cheese
1 tablespoon mayonnaise
1 tablespoon lemon juice
2 teaspoons dry ranch salad
    dressing mix
1 can (3 ounces) chunk light tuna
    packed in water, drained and
    flaked
2 tablespoons sliced green onion
    or chopped celery
1 teaspoon dried parsley flakes
1 package (12 ounces) baby
    carrots

1. Combine cottage cheese, mayonnaise, lemon juice and salad dressing mix in food processor or blender. Process until smooth.

2. Combine tuna, green onion and parsley flakes in small bowl. Stir in cottage cheese mixture. Serve with carrots.

Makes 4 servings

Lunchbox Delights

Grilled Roasted Red Pepper & Mozzarella Sandwich

1 tablespoon olive oil vinaigrette or Italian salad dressing
2 slices (1 ounce each) Italian-style sandwich bread
  Fresh basil leaves (optional)
⅓ cup roasted red peppers, rinsed, drained and patted dry
1 to 2 slices (1 ounce each) mozzarella or Swiss cheese
  Olive oil cooking spray

1. Brush vinaigrette on 1 side of 1 bread slice; top with basil, if desired, peppers, cheese and remaining bread slice.

2. Lightly spray both sides of sandwich with cooking spray.

3. Heat large nonstick skillet over medium heat. Add sandwich; cook 4 to 5 minutes per side or until cheese melts and sandwich is golden brown.

Makes 1 sandwich

Kids' Quesadillas

8 slices American cheese
8 (10-inch) flour tortillas
½ pound thinly sliced deli turkey
6 tablespoons *French's*® Honey Mustard
2 tablespoons melted butter
¼ teaspoon paprika

1. To prepare 1 quesadilla, arrange 2 slices of cheese on 1 tortilla. Top with ¼ of turkey. Spread with 1½ *tablespoons* mustard, then top with another tortilla. Prepare 3 more quesadillas with remaining ingredients.

2. Combine butter and paprika. Brush one side of tortilla with butter mixture. Preheat 12-inch nonstick skillet over medium-high heat. Place tortilla, butter side down, and cook 2 minutes. Brush top of tortilla with butter mixture and turn over. Cook 1½ minutes or until golden brown. Repeat with remaining 3 quesadillas.

3. Slice into wedges before serving.   *Makes 4 servings*

Prep Time: 5 minutes • Cook Time: 15 minutes

Silly Snake Sandwich

8 tablespoons peanut butter, divided
1 loaf (½ pound) sliced French or Italian bread, about 11 inches long
    and 3 inches wide
1 (2-inch) red bell pepper strip
1 black olive, cut in half lengthwise
1 green olive, chopped
½ cup jelly, any flavor
¼ cup marshmallow creme

1. Using 1 tablespoon peanut butter, attach first 2 inches (3 to 4 slices) bread loaf together to make snake head. Cut bell pepper strip into tongue shape by cutting a small triangle out of one end. (See photo.) Make very small horizontal slice in heel of bread, being careful not to cut all the way through. Place "tongue" into slice. Attach black olive slices with peanut butter to snake head for eyes. Attach 2 green olive pieces with peanut butter for nostrils. Set snake head aside.

2. Combine remaining peanut butter, jelly and marshmallow creme in small bowl until smooth. Spread on half of bread slices; top with remaining bread slices.

3. Place snake head on large serving tray. Arrange sandwiches in wavy pattern to resemble slithering snake. Serve immediately.

Makes about 8 small sandwiches

Funny Face Sandwich Melts

2 super-size English muffins, split and toasted
8 teaspoons *French's*® Honey Mustard
1 can (8 ounces) crushed pineapple, drained
8 ounces sliced smoked ham
4 slices Swiss cheese or white American cheese

1. Place English muffins, cut side up, on baking sheet. Spread each with *2 teaspoons* mustard. Arrange one-fourth of the pineapple, ham and cheese on top, dividing evenly.

2. Broil until cheese melts, about 1 minute. Decorate with mustard and assorted vegetables to create your own funny face. *Makes 4 servings*

Tip: This sandwich is also easy to prepare in the toaster oven.

Prep Time: 10 minutes • Cook Time: 1 minute

Mexican Pita Pile-Ups

4 small (4-inch) rounds whole wheat pita bread
1 cup shredded cooked chicken breast
¼ cup canned chopped mild green chiles, drained
1 tablespoon fresh lime juice
1 teaspoon ground cumin
1 cup chopped seeded fresh tomato
¼ cup chopped fresh cilantro (optional)
1 can (2¼ ounces) sliced black olives, drained
1 cup (4 ounces) shredded sharp Cheddar cheese

MICROWAVE DIRECTIONS

1. Place pitas on microwavable plates. Combine chicken, chiles, lime juice and cumin in medium bowl.

2. Top pitas evenly with chicken mixture, tomato, cilantro, if desired, olives and cheese.

3. Microwave each pile-up on HIGH 1 minute or until cheese is melted. Let stand 2 to 3 minutes before serving.   *Makes 4 servings*

Croque Monsieur

8 slices firm white sandwich bread
2 tablespoons butter, softened
8 slices SARGENTO® Deli Style Sliced Swiss Cheese
2 tablespoons honey mustard
4 slices CURE 81® ham
4 slices cooked turkey breast

1. Spread one side of each slice of bread with butter; place buttered side down on waxed paper. Top each of 4 slices of bread with 1 slice of cheese. Spread mustard over cheese; top with ham, turkey and remaining slices of cheese. Close sandwiches with remaining 4 slices of bread, buttered side up.

2. Heat large skillet or griddle over medium heat until hot. Cook sandwiches in batches in skillet or on griddle until golden brown, about 3 minutes per side.

Makes 4 servings

Prep Time: 8 minutes • Cook Time: 6 minutes

Broccoli-Cheese Quesadillas

1 cup (4 ounces) shredded
    Cheddar cheese
½ cup finely chopped fresh
    broccoli
2 tablespoons salsa or picante
    sauce
4 (6- to 7-inch) corn or flour
    tortillas
1 teaspoon butter, divided

1. Combine cheese, broccoli and salsa in small bowl; mix well.

2. Spoon one fourth of cheese mixture onto 1 side of each tortilla; fold tortilla over filling.

3. Melt ½ teaspoon butter in large nonstick skillet over medium heat. Add 2 quesadillas; cook about 2 minutes per side or until tortillas are golden brown and cheese is melted. Repeat with remaining butter and quesadillas.

Makes 4 servings

Tip: Refrigerate individually wrapped quesadillas up to 2 days or freeze up to 3 weeks.

Tuna Schooners

1 can (6 ounces) tuna, packed in water, drained and flaked
½ cup finely chopped apple
¼ cup shredded carrot
⅓ cup ranch salad dressing
2 English muffins, split and lightly toasted
8 triangular-shaped tortilla chips or triangular-shaped baked whole wheat crackers

1. Combine tuna, apple and carrot in medium bowl. Add salad dressing; mix well.

2. Spread one fourth of tuna mixture on each muffin half.

3. Stand 2 chips and press firmly into tuna mixture on each muffin half to form sails.

Makes 4 servings

Monster Sandwiches

8 assorted round and oblong sandwich rolls
Butter
16 to 24 slices assorted cold cuts (salami, turkey, ham and/or bologna)
6 to 8 slices assorted cheeses (American, Swiss and/or Muenster)
1 firm tomato, sliced
1 cucumber, sliced thinly
Assorted lettuce leaves (Romaine, curly and/or red leaf)
Cocktail onions, green and black olives, cherry tomatoes, pickled gherkins, radishes, baby corn and/or hard-boiled eggs

1. Cut rolls open just below center; spread with butter.

2. Layer meats, cheeses, tomato, cucumber and greens to make monster faces. Roll tongues from ham slices or make lips with tomato slices.

3. Use toothpicks to affix remaining ingredients for eyes, ears, fins, horns and hair as shown in photo. *Makes 8 sandwiches*

Note: Remember to remove toothpicks before eating. Or substitute pretzel sticks for the toothpicks.

Tasty Turkey Turnovers

1 package (about 11 ounces) refrigerated dinner rolls
2 tablespoons honey mustard, plus additional for dipping
3 ounces sliced deli turkey breast
¾ cup packaged broccoli coleslaw
1 egg white, beaten

1. Preheat oven to 425°F. Spray baking sheet with nonstick cooking spray.

2. Separate dinner rolls; place on lightly floured surface. Roll each dinner roll into 3½-inch circle with lightly floured rolling pin. Spread honey mustard lightly over dinner rolls; top with turkey and broccoli coleslaw. Brush edges of dinner rolls with egg white. Fold dough in half; press edges with tines of fork to seal.

3. Place turnovers on prepared baking sheet; brush with egg white. Bake about 15 minutes or until golden brown. Let stand 5 minutes before serving. Serve with additional mustard for dipping.   *Makes 8 servings*

Tangy Italian Chicken Sandwiches

2 cups (8 ounces) chopped cooked boneless skinless chicken breast
⅓ cup drained giardiniera
2 ounces provolone cheese slices, diced
¼ cup chopped fresh parsley
3 tablespoons Italian salad dressing
¼ teaspoon dried oregano
4 small (4-inch) rounds pita bread, cut in half crosswise
8 leaves romaine or red leaf lettuce

1. Combine chicken, giardiniera, cheese, parsley, dressing and oregano in medium bowl; mix well.

2. Line each pita half with lettuce leaf.

3. Divide chicken mixture evenly among pita pockets.

Makes 4 servings

Prep Time: 15 minutes

Backbones

4 (10-inch) flour tortillas
1 package (3½ ounces) soft cheese spread with herbs
1 bag (6 ounces) fresh baby spinach
½ pound thinly sliced salami or ham
½ pound thinly sliced Havarti or Swiss cheese
1 jar (7 ounces) roasted red bell peppers, drained and sliced into
**   thin strips**

1. Spread 1 tortilla with 2 to 3 tablespoons cheese spread. Layer evenly with one fourth of spinach, salami and cheese. Place bell pepper strips down center.

2. Tightly roll up. Slice off and discard rounded ends, if desired. Repeat with remaining tortillas and filling ingredients.

3. Cut tortilla rolls into 1½-inch slices; secure with toothpicks. To serve, stack slices in twos or threes on serving plate.   *Makes 18 servings*

Zippity Hot Doggity Tacos

1 small onion, finely chopped
1 tablespoon *Frank's*® *RedHot*® Original Cayenne Pepper Sauce or
    ***French's*® Worcestershire Sauce**
4 frankfurters, chopped
1 can (about 15 ounces) red kidney or black beans, drained
1 can (8 ounces) tomato sauce
1 teaspoon chili powder
8 taco shells, heated
1 cup *French's*® French Fried Onions
    Garnish: chopped tomatoes, shredded lettuce, sliced olives, sour
    cream, shredded cheese

1. Heat *1 tablespoon oil* in 12-inch nonstick skillet over medium-high heat. Cook onion 3 minutes or until crisp-tender. Stir in remaining ingredients. Bring to a boil. Reduce heat to medium-low and cook 5 minutes, stirring occasionally.

2. To serve, spoon chili into taco shells. Garnish as desired and sprinkle with French Fried Onions. Splash on *Frank's RedHot* Sauce for extra zip!

Makes 4 servings

Prep Time: 5 minutes • Cook Time: 8 minutes

Grilled Cheese & Turkey Shapes

8 teaspoons *French's*® Mustard, any flavor
8 slices seedless rye or sourdough bread
8 slices deli roast turkey
4 slices American cheese
2 tablespoons butter or margarine, softened

1. Spread *1 teaspoon* mustard on each slice of bread. Arrange turkey and cheese on half of the bread slices, dividing evenly. Cover with remaining slices of bread.

2. Cut out sandwich shapes using cookie cutters. Remove excess trimmings.

3. Spread butter on both sides of sandwich. Heat large nonstick skillet over medium heat. Cook sandwiches 1 minute per side or until bread is golden and cheese melts. *Makes 4 sandwiches*

Tip: Use 2½-inch star, heart, teddy bear or flower-shaped cookie cutters.

Prep Time: 15 minutes • Cook Time: 2 minutes

Kids' Wraps

   4 teaspoons Dijon honey mustard
   2 (8-inch) flour tortillas
   2 slices American cheese, cut in half
   4 ounces sliced oven-roasted turkey breast
   ½ cup shredded carrot (about 1 medium)
   3 romaine lettuce leaves, washed and torn into bite-size pieces

1. Spread 2 teaspoons mustard evenly over each tortilla.

2. Top each tortilla with 2 cheese halves, half of turkey, half of carrot and half of lettuce.

3. Roll up tortillas; cut in half.   *Makes 2 servings*

What's for Dinner

Cheeseburger Calzones

- **1 pound ground beef**
- **1 medium onion, chopped**
- **½ teaspoon salt**
- **1 jar (1 pound 10 ounces) RAGÚ® Chunky Pasta Sauce**
- **1 jar (8 ounces) marinated mushrooms, drained and chopped (optional)**
- **1 cup shredded Cheddar cheese (about 4 ounces)**
- **1 package (12 ounces) refrigerated large flaky biscuits (8 biscuits)**

1. Preheat oven to 375°F. In 12-inch skillet, brown ground beef with onion and salt over medium-high heat; drain. Stir in 1 cup Ragú Pasta Sauce, mushrooms and cheese.

2. Roll or press out each biscuit into a 6-inch circle. Place ½ cup beef mixture on each dough circle; fold over and press edges to close. Seal completely by pressing firmly along edges with the tines of a fork.

3. With large spatula, gently arrange on cookie sheets. Bake 13 minutes or until golden. Serve with remaining sauce, heated.   *Makes 8 servings*

Prep Time: 20 minutes • Cook Time: 13 minutes

Mexican Tortilla Stack-Ups

1 tablespoon vegetable oil
½ cup chopped onion
1 can (about 15 ounces) black beans, rinsed and drained
1 can (about 14 ounces) Mexican-style diced tomatoes, undrained
1 cup frozen corn
1 envelope (1¼ ounces) taco seasoning mix
6 (6-inch) corn tortillas
2 cups (8 ounces) taco-flavored shredded Cheddar cheese
1 cup water
   Sour cream (optional)
   Sliced black olives (optional)

1. Preheat oven to 350°F. Spray 13×9-inch baking dish with nonstick cooking spray. Heat oil in large skillet over medium-high heat. Add onion; cook and stir 3 minutes or until tender. Add beans, tomatoes with juice, corn and taco seasoning mix. Bring to a boil over high heat. Reduce heat to low and simmer 5 minutes.

2. Place 2 tortillas side by side in prepared dish. Top each tortilla with about ½ cup bean mixture. Sprinkle evenly with one third of cheese. Repeat layers twice, creating 2 tortilla stacks, each 3 tortillas high. Pour water along sides of tortillas.

3. Cover tightly with foil; bake 30 to 35 minutes or until heated through. Cut stacks into wedges. Serve with sour cream and black olives, if desired. *Makes 6 servings*

Ham & Cheese Shells & Trees

2 tablespoons margarine or butter
1 (6.2-ounce) package PASTA RONI® Shells & White Cheddar
2 cups fresh or frozen chopped broccoli
⅔ cup milk
1½ cups ham or cooked turkey, cut into thin strips (about 6 ounces)

1. In large saucepan, bring 2 cups water and margarine to a boil.

2. Stir in pasta. Reduce heat to medium. Gently boil, uncovered, 6 minutes, stirring occasionally. Stir in broccoli; return to a boil. Boil 6 to 8 minutes or until most of water is absorbed.

3. Stir in milk, ham and Special Seasonings. Return to a boil; boil 1 to 2 minutes or until pasta is tender. Let stand 5 minutes before serving.

Makes 4 servings

Tip: No leftovers? Ask the deli to slice a ½-inch-thick piece of ham or turkey.

Prep Time: 5 minutes • Cook Time: 20 minutes

Tuna Monte Cristo Sandwiches

4 slices Cheddar cheese
4 slices sourdough or challah (egg) bread
½ pound deli tuna salad
¼ cup milk
1 egg
2 tablespoons butter

1. Place 1 slice cheese on each of 2 bread slices. Spread tuna salad evenly over cheese. Top with remaining cheese and bread slices.

2. Combine milk and egg in shallow bowl; beat until well blended. Dip sandwiches in egg mixture, turning to coat well.

3. Melt butter in large nonstick skillet over medium heat. Add sandwiches; cook 4 to 5 minutes per side or until cheese melts and sandwiches are golden brown. *Makes 2 servings*

Serving Suggestion: Serve with a chilled fruit salad.

Prep and Cook Time: 20 minutes

Golden Chicken Nuggets

1 pound boneless skinless chicken, cut into 1½-inch pieces
¼ cup *French's*® Honey Mustard
2 cups *French's*® French Fried Onions, finely crushed

1. Preheat oven to 400°F. Toss chicken with mustard in medium bowl.

2. Place French Fried Onions into resealable plastic food storage bag. Toss chicken in onions, a few pieces at a time, pressing gently to adhere.

3. Place nuggets in shallow baking pan. Bake 15 minutes or until chicken is no longer pink in center. Serve with additional honey mustard.   *Makes 4 servings*

Prep Time: 5 minutes • Cook Time: 15 minutes

Kid's Choice Meatballs

1½ pounds ground beef
¼ cup dry seasoned bread crumbs
¼ cup grated Parmesan cheese
3 tablespoons *French's*® Worcestershire Sauce
1 egg
2 jars (14 ounces each) spaghetti sauce

1. Preheat oven to 425°F. In bowl, gently mix beef, bread crumbs, cheese, Worcestershire and egg. Shape into 1-inch meatballs. Place on rack in roasting pan. Bake 15 minutes or until cooked.

2. In large saucepan, combine meatballs and spaghetti sauce. Cook until heated through. Serve over cooked pasta.

Makes 6 to 8 servings
(about 48 meatballs)

Quick Meatball Tip: On waxed paper, pat meat mixture into 8×6×1-inch rectangle. With knife, cut crosswise and lengthwise into 1-inch rows. Roll each small square into a ball.

Prep Time: 10 minutes • Cook Time: 20 minutes

Taco Pizza

Nonstick cooking spray
1 package (about 14 ounces) refrigerated pizza dough
¾ pound ground turkey
½ cup chopped onion
1 can (8 ounces) tomato sauce
1 envelope (1¼ ounces) taco seasoning mix
2 medium plum tomatoes, thinly sliced
1 cup (4 ounces) shredded Cheddar cheese
1½ cups shredded lettuce

1. Preheat oven to 425°F. Lightly spray 12-inch pizza pan with cooking spray. Unroll pizza dough; press into prepared pan. Build up edges slightly. Prick dough with fork. Bake 7 to 10 minutes or until lightly browned.

2. Meanwhile, lightly spray large nonstick skillet with cooking spray. Add turkey and onion; cook and stir until turkey is no longer pink. Add tomato sauce and taco seasoning; bring to a boil. Reduce heat; simmer, uncovered, 2 to 3 minutes. Spoon turkey mixture on warm pizza crust. Bake 5 minutes.

3. Arrange tomatoes over turkey mixture. Sprinkle with cheese. Bake 2 to 3 minutes or until cheese melts. Top with lettuce. Cut into 8 slices.

Makes 4 servings

Prep Time: 15 minutes • Bake Time: 7 to 8 minutes

Easy Chicken & Rice Wraps

   1 (6.8-ounce) package RICE-A-RONI® Spanish Rice
   2 tablespoons margarine or butter
   1 (16-ounce) jar salsa*
 12 ounces boneless, skinless chicken breasts, cut into thin strips
     (about 3 breasts)
   1 cup canned black or red kidney beans, drained and rinsed
   1 cup frozen or canned corn, drained
   8 (6-inch) flour tortillas, warmed
     Shredded Cheddar cheese and sour cream (optional)

*Or use 2 cups chopped fresh tomatoes or 1 (14½-ounce) can tomatoes, undrained and chopped, if desired.

1. In large skillet over medium-high heat, sauté rice-vermicelli mix with margarine until vermicelli is golden brown.

2. Slowly stir in 2 cups water, salsa, chicken and Special Seasonings; bring to a boil. Reduce heat to low. Cover; simmer 15 to 20 minutes or until rice is tender and chicken is no longer pink inside.

3. Stir in beans and corn; let stand 5 minutes before serving. Serve in tortillas with cheese and sour cream, if desired.　　　*Makes 4 servings*

Tip: To warm tortillas, wrap them in aluminum foil and bake in a 350°F oven for about 5 minutes. Turn off the heat and keep them in the oven until ready to serve.

Prep Time: 10 minutes • Cook Time: 30 minutes

Zesty Meatball Sandwiches

1 jar (16 ounces) spicy thick and chunky salsa
1 can (8 ounces) tomato sauce
1 to 2 teaspoons chili powder or chipotle chili powder
1 pound ground beef
⅓ cup plain dry bread crumbs
¼ cup minced onion
1 egg
½ teaspoon salt
½ teaspoon black pepper
4 (6-inch) sourdough or French rolls, split

1. Combine salsa, tomato sauce and chili powder in medium bowl; set aside.

2. Combine beef, bread crumbs, onion, egg, salt and pepper in large bowl; mix well. Shape into 16 (1½-inch) meatballs.

3. Brown meatballs 6 to 8 minutes in large skillet over medium-high heat. Drain fat. Add salsa mixture; bring to a boil. Cover; reduce heat to low. Cook 20 to 25 minutes, stirring occasionally. Place 4 meatballs in each roll; top with salsa mixture. *Makes 4 servings*

Surfin' Salmon

⅓ **cup cornflake crumbs**
⅓ **cup cholesterol-free egg substitute**
 2 **tablespoons milk**
¾ **teaspoon dried dill weed**
⅛ **teaspoon black pepper**
   Dash hot pepper sauce
 1 **can (about 14 ounces) salmon, drained, skin and bones removed**
   Nonstick cooking spray
 1 **teaspoon olive oil**
 6 **tablespoons tartar sauce**
 1 **tablespoon diced pimiento**

1. Combine cornflake crumbs, egg substitute, milk, dill, black pepper and hot pepper sauce in large bowl. Add salmon; mix well. Shape salmon mixture into 5 large egg-shaped balls. Flatten each ball into ¾-inch-thick oval. Pinch one end of each oval to make tail shape.

2. Spray large nonstick skillet with cooking spray. Cook fish over medium-high heat 2 to 3 minutes per side or until firm and lightly browned. Add oil to skillet, as necessary, to prevent sticking and increase browning.

3. Place small drop tartar sauce and 1 piece pimiento on each fish to make eye. Serve with remaining tartar sauce, if desired.

Makes 5 servings

Serving Suggestion: For a tasty side dish of sea plants, serve fish on a bed of shredded Romaine lettuce and matchstick-size cucumber slices.

Make Your Own Pizza Shapes

1 package (10 ounces) refrigerated pizza dough
¼ to ½ cup prepared pizza sauce
1 cup shredded mozzarella cheese
1 cup *French's*® French Fried Onions

1. Preheat oven to 425°F. Unroll dough onto greased baking sheet. Press or roll dough into 12×8-inch rectangle. With sharp knife or pizza cutter, cut dough into large shape of your choice (butterfly, heart, star). Reroll scraps and cut into mini shapes. (See tip.)

2. Pre-bake crust 7 minutes or until crust just begins to brown. Spread with sauce and top with cheese. Bake 6 minutes or until crust is deep golden brown.

3. Sprinkle with French Fried Onions. Bake 2 minutes longer or until golden.   *Makes 4 to 6 servings*

Tip: Pizza dough can be cut with 6-inch shaped cookie cutters. Spread with sauce and top with cheese. Bake about 10 minutes or until crust is golden. Sprinkle with French Fried Onions. Bake 2 minutes longer.

Prep Time: 10 minutes • Cook Time: 15 minutes

Traditional Spaghetti Sauce

12 ounces spaghetti
1 pound mild Italian sausage
½ cup chopped onion
1 can (14.5 ounces) CONTADINA® Recipe Ready Diced Tomatoes with Roasted Garlic, undrained
1 cup chicken broth or water
1 can (6 ounces) CONTADINA Italian Paste with Italian Seasonings
1 tablespoon chopped fresh parsley

1. Cook pasta according to package directions; drain and keep warm.

2. Crumble sausage into large skillet. Cook over medium-high heat, stirring to break up sausage, 4 to 5 minutes or until no longer pink.

3. Add onion; cook 2 to 3 minutes. Drain.

4. Stir in undrained tomatoes, broth, tomato paste and parsley. Bring to a boil. Reduce heat; cook 10 to 15 minutes or until flavors are blended. Serve sauce over pasta. *Makes 4 to 6 servings*

Octo-Dogs and Shells

4 hot dogs
1½ cups uncooked small shell pasta
1½ cups frozen mixed vegetables
1 cup prepared Alfredo sauce
Prepared mustard
Cheese-flavored fish-shaped crackers

1. Lay 1 hot dog on cutting surface. Starting 1 inch from one end of hot dog, slice hot dog vertically in half. Roll hot dog ¼ turn. Starting 1 inch from same end, slice in half vertically again, making 4 segments connected at top. Slice each segment in half vertically, creating total of 8 legs. Repeat with remaining hot dogs.

2. Place hot dogs in medium saucepan; cover with water. Bring to a boil over medium-high heat.

3. Meanwhile, prepare pasta according to package directions, stirring in vegetables during last 3 minutes of cooking time. Drain; return to pan. Stir in Alfredo sauce. Heat over low heat until heated through. Divide pasta mixture between 4 plates. Drain octo-dogs. Arrange one octo-dog on top of pasta mixture on each plate. Draw faces on heads of octo-dogs with mustard. Sprinkle crackers over pasta. *Makes 4 servings*

Shredded BBQ Chicken Sandwiches

    1 jar (1 pound 10 ounces) RAGÚ® Old World Style® Pasta Sauce
    3 tablespoons firmly packed brown sugar
    2 tablespoons apple cider vinegar
1½ tablespoons chili powder
    2 teaspoons garlic powder
1½ teaspoons onion powder
    4 boneless, skinless chicken breast halves (about 1¼ pounds)
    6 hamburger buns or round rolls

1. In 6-quart saucepot, cook Ragú Pasta Sauce, brown sugar, vinegar, chili powder, garlic powder and onion powder over medium heat, stirring occasionally, 5 minutes.

2. Season chicken, if desired, with salt and ground black pepper. Add chicken to sauce. Reduce heat to medium-low and simmer, covered, stirring occasionally, 20 minutes or until chicken is no longer pink in center. Remove saucepot from heat.

3. Remove chicken from sauce. Using two forks, shred chicken. Return shredded chicken to sauce and heat through. To serve, arrange chicken mixture on buns and garnish, if desired, with shredded Cheddar cheese.

Makes 6 servings

Prep Time: 5 minutes • Cook Time: 30 minutes

Salsa Macaroni & Cheese

**1 jar (1 pound) RAGÚ® Cheesy!
Double Cheddar Sauce
1 cup prepared mild salsa
8 ounces elbow macaroni, cooked
and drained**

1. In 2-quart saucepan, heat Ragú Double Cheddar Sauce over medium heat. Stir in salsa; heat through.

2. Toss with hot macaroni. Serve immediately. *Makes 4 servings*

Prep Time: 5 minutes • Cook Time: 15 minutes

Campfire Hot Dogs

½ pound ground beef
2 cups RAGÚ® Old World Style®
Pasta Sauce
1 can (10¾ to 16 ounces) baked
beans
8 frankfurters, cooked
8 frankfurter rolls

1. In 12-inch skillet, brown ground beef over medium-high heat; drain.

2. Stir in Ragú Pasta Sauce and beans. Bring to a boil over high heat. Reduce heat to low and simmer, stirring occasionally, 5 minutes.

3. To serve, arrange frankfurters in rolls and top with sauce mixture. Garnish, if desired, with Cheddar cheese.   *Makes 8 servings*

Tip: For Chili Campfire Hot Dogs, simply stir 2 to 3 teaspoons chili powder into sauce mixture.

Prep Time: 5 minutes • Cook Time: 10 minutes

Little Piggy Pies

2 cups frozen mixed vegetables
1 can (10¾ ounces) condensed cream of chicken soup, undiluted
8 ounces chopped cooked chicken
⅓ cup plain yogurt
⅓ cup water
½ teaspoon dried thyme
¼ teaspoon poultry seasoning or ground sage
⅛ teaspoon garlic powder
1 package (10 biscuits) refrigerated flaky buttermilk biscuit dough

1. Preheat oven to 400°F. Remove 10 peas from frozen mixed vegetables; set aside. Combine remaining vegetables, soup, chicken, yogurt, water, thyme, poultry seasoning and garlic powder in medium saucepan. Bring to a boil, stirring frequently. Cover; keep warm.

2. Press 5 biscuits into 3-inch circles. Cut remaining 5 biscuits into 8 wedges each. Place 2 wedges on top of each circle; fold down points to form ears. Roll 5 wedges into small balls; place in centers to form snouts. Use tip of spoon handle to make nostrils. Use reserved peas to form eyes.

3. Spoon hot chicken mixture into 5 (10-ounce) custard cups. Place a biscuit pig on top of each. Place remaining biscuit wedges around each pig, twisting 1 wedge for tail. Bake 10 to 12 minutes or until pigs are golden brown. *Makes 5 servings*

Twice Baked Potatoes

3 hot baked potatoes, split lengthwise
½ cup sour cream
2 tablespoons butter or margarine
1⅓ cups *French's*® French Fried Onions, divided
1 cup (4 ounces) shredded Cheddar cheese, divided
Dash paprika (optional)

1. Preheat oven to 400°F. Scoop out insides of potatoes into medium bowl, leaving thin shells. Mash potatoes with sour cream and butter until smooth. Stir in ⅔ *cup* French Fried Onions and ½ *cup* cheese. Spoon mixture into shells.

2. Bake 20 minutes or until heated through. Top with remaining cheese, onions and paprika, if desired. Bake 2 minutes or until cheese melts.

Makes 6 servings

Tip: To bake potatoes quickly, microwave on HIGH 10 to 12 minutes or until tender.

Variation: For added Cheddar flavor, substitute *French's*® Cheddar French Fried Onions for the original flavor.

Prep Time: 10 minutes • Cook Time: 22 minutes

Mini Mexican Burger Bites

1½ **pounds ground beef**
½ **cup finely chopped red, yellow or green bell pepper**
2 **tablespoons** *French's*® **Worcestershire Sauce**
1 **teaspoon** *Frank's*® *RedHot*® **Original Cayenne Pepper Sauce**
1 **teaspoon dried oregano leaves**
¼ **teaspoon salt**
12 **mini dinner rolls**
  Shredded Cheddar cheese
  Shredded lettuce (optional)

1. Gently combine all ingredients except rolls, cheese and lettuce in large bowl. Shape into 12 mini patties. Broil or grill patties 4 to 6 minutes for medium doneness (160°F internal temperature), turning once.

2. Arrange burgers on rolls and top with Cheddar cheese. Top with shredded lettuce. *Makes 6 servings*

Prep Time: 5 minutes • Cook Time: 8 minutes

Sweet Treats

Chocolate Malt Delights

1 package (16 ounces) refrigerated chocolate chip cookie dough
⅓ cup plus 3 tablespoons malted milk powder, original or chocolate flavor, divided
1¼ cups prepared chocolate frosting
1 cup coarsely chopped malted milk balls

1. Preheat oven to 350°F. Grease cookie sheets. Let dough stand at room temperature about 15 minutes.

2. Beat dough and ⅓ cup malted milk powder in large bowl with electric mixer at medium speed until well blended. Drop rounded tablespoonfuls of dough onto prepared cookie sheets. Bake 10 to 12 minutes or until edges are lightly browned. Cool 5 minutes on cookie sheets. Remove to wire racks; cool completely.

3. Combine frosting and remaining 3 tablespoons malted milk powder. Top each cookie with rounded tablespoonful of frosting; garnish with malted milk balls. *Makes about 1½ dozen cookies*

Flapjack Party Stack

1 package (about 18 ounces) yellow cake mix, plus ingredients to prepare mix
1 container (16 ounces) vanilla frosting
1 quart fresh strawberries, hulled and sliced
1 cup caramel or butterscotch ice cream topping

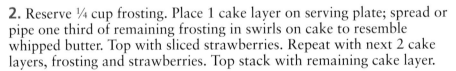

1. Preheat oven to 350°F. Grease 4 (9-inch) round cake pans; line with waxed paper. Prepare cake mix according to package directions; divide evenly between prepared pans. Bake according to package directions, adjusting baking time as necessary. Cool cake layers 15 minutes in pans on wire racks. Remove from pans to racks; cool completely.

2. Reserve ¼ cup frosting. Place 1 cake layer on serving plate; spread or pipe one third of remaining frosting in swirls on cake to resemble whipped butter. Top with sliced strawberries. Repeat with next 2 cake layers, frosting and strawberries. Top stack with remaining cake layer.

3. Heat caramel topping in microwave just until pourable. Drizzle over cake. Spread or pipe reserved frosting in center; garnish with remaining strawberries.   *Makes 12 servings*

Cookie Sundae Cups

1 package (about 16 ounces) refrigerated chocolate chip cookie dough
6 cups (1½ quarts) ice cream, any flavor
Ice cream topping, any flavor
Whipped topping
Colored sprinkles

1. Preheat oven to 350°F. Lightly grease 18 standard (2½-inch) muffin cups. Shape dough into 18 balls; press onto bottoms and up sides of prepared muffin cups.

2. Bake 14 to 18 minutes or until golden brown. Cool in pans on wire racks 10 minutes. Remove from pans to racks; cool completely.

3. Place ⅓ cup ice cream in each cookie cup. Drizzle with ice cream topping. Top with whipped topping and sprinkles.

Makes 1½ dozen sundae cups

Chocolate Banana Cake

CAKE

> 1 package DUNCAN HINES® Moist Deluxe® Devil's Food Cake Mix
> 3 eggs
> 1⅓ cups milk
> ½ cup vegetable oil

TOPPING

> 1 package (4-serving size) banana cream instant pudding and
>   pie filling mix
> 1 cup milk
> 1 cup whipping cream, whipped
> 1 medium banana
>   Lemon juice
>   Chocolate sprinkles for garnish

1. Preheat oven to 350°F. Grease and flour 13×9×2-inch pan.

2. For cake, combine cake mix, eggs, milk and oil in large bowl. Beat at low speed with electric mixer until moistened. Beat at medium speed 2 minutes. Pour into pan. Bake at 350°F for 35 to 38 minutes or until toothpick inserted in center comes out clean. Cool completely.

3. For topping, combine pudding mix and milk in large bowl. Stir until smooth. Fold in whipped cream. Spread on top of cooled cake. Slice banana; dip in lemon juice and arrange on top. Garnish with chocolate sprinkles. Refrigerate until ready to serve.   *Makes 12 to 16 servings*

Tip: A wire whisk is a great utensil to use when making instant pudding. It quickly eliminates all lumps.

Cubcakes

   1 package (about 18 ounces) chocolate cake mix, plus ingredients to
      prepare mix
   1 container (16 ounces) chocolate frosting
   1 package (5 ounces) chocolate nonpareil candies
  72 red cinnamon candies
     Chocolate sprinkles
     Black decorating gel

1. Line 24 standard (2½-inch) muffin cups with paper baking cups or spray with nonstick cooking spray.

2. Prepare cake mix and bake in prepared pans according to package directions. Cool cupcakes 15 minutes in pans on wire racks. Remove from pans to racks; cool completely.

3. Frost cooled cupcakes with chocolate frosting. Use nonpareils to create ears and muzzle. Add cinnamon candies for eyes. Decorate with chocolate sprinkles for fur. Use decorating gel to place dots on eyes, create mouth and attach cinnamon candy for nose.

Makes 24 cupcakes

Peanut Butter and Milk Chocolate Chip Clusters

1 cup HERSHEY'S Milk Chocolate Chips
1 cup REESE'S® Peanut Butter Chips
2 teaspoons shortening (do not use butter, margarine, spread or oil)
2 cups peanuts

1. Place milk chocolate chips, peanut butter chips and shortening in medium microwave-safe bowl. Microwave at MEDIUM (50%) 1 minute; stir. If necessary, microwave at MEDIUM an additional 15 seconds at a time, stirring after each heating, just until chips are melted and mixture is smooth when stirred. Stir in peanuts.

2. Spoon heaping teaspoons of peanut mixture into 1-inch paper candy cups or paper-lined muffin cups. Refrigerate 1 hour or until firm. Store tightly covered in refrigerator.   *Makes about 2½ dozen candies*

Christmas Mouse Ice Creams

2 cups vanilla ice cream
1 package (4 ounces) single-
    serving graham cracker crusts
6 chocolate sandwich cookies,
    separated and cream filling
    removed
12 black jelly beans
  6 red jelly beans
36 chocolate sprinkles
    (approximately ¼ teaspoon)

1. Place 1 rounded scoop (about ⅓ cup) ice cream into each crust. Freeze 10 minutes.

2. Press 1 cookie half into each side of ice cream scoops for ears. Decorate with black jelly beans for eyes, red jelly beans for noses and chocolate sprinkles for whiskers.

3. Freeze 10 minutes before serving.

Makes 6 servings

Chocolate Bunny Cookies

1 (21-ounce) package DUNCAN HINES® Family-Style Chewy Fudge
    Brownie Mix
1 egg
¼ cup water
¼ cup vegetable oil
1⅓ cups pecan halves (96)
1 container DUNCAN HINES® Creamy Home-Style Dark Chocolate
    Fudge Frosting
White chocolate chips

1. Preheat oven to 350°F. Grease baking sheets.

2. Combine brownie mix, egg, water and oil in large bowl. Stir with spoon until well blended, about 50 strokes. Drop by level tablespoonfuls 2 inches apart on greased baking sheets. Place two pecan halves, flat side up, on each cookie for ears. Bake at 350°F for 10 to 12 minutes or until set. Cool 2 minutes on baking sheets. Remove to cooling racks. Cool completely.

3. Spread Dark Chocolate Fudge frosting on one cookie. Place white chocolate chips, upside down, on frosting for eyes and nose. Dot each eye with frosting using toothpick. Repeat with remaining cookies. Allow frosting to set before storing cookies between layers of waxed paper in airtight container. *Makes 4 dozen cookies*

Tip: For variety, frost cookies with Duncan Hines® Vanilla Frosting and use semisweet chocolate chips for the eyes and noses.

Peanut Butter Cup Cookie Ice Cream Pie

½ cup creamy peanut butter
¼ cup honey
1 cup KEEBLER® Chips Deluxe™ Peanut Butter Cups Cookies
  (about 8 cookies)
1 quart vanilla ice cream, softened
1 KEEBLER® Ready-Crust® Chocolate Pie Crust
½ cup chocolate ice cream topping

1. Place large bowl in freezer.

2. In small bowl, stir together peanut butter and honey. Set aside. Coarsely chop cookies.

3. In chilled bowl, combine ice cream, peanut butter mixture and cookies. Beat on low speed of electric mixer until combined. Spread half of ice cream mixture in crust.

4. Drizzle with ice cream topping. Carefully spread remaining ice cream mixture on top. Freeze at least 3 hours or until firm.

5. Let stand at room temperature for 15 minutes before cutting. Garnish as desired. Store in freezer.   *Makes 8 servings*

Prep Time: 15 minutes • Freeze Time: 3 hours

Play Ball

  2 cups plus 1 tablespoon all-purpose flour, divided
  ¾ cup granulated sugar
  ¾ cup packed brown sugar
  1 tablespoon baking powder
  1 teaspoon salt
  ½ teaspoon baking soda
  1¼ cups milk
  3 eggs
  ½ cup shortening
  1½ teaspoons vanilla
  ½ cup mini semisweet chocolate chips
  1 container (16 ounces) vanilla frosting
  Assorted candies and food colorings

1. Preheat oven to 350°F. Line 24 standard (2½-inch) muffin cups with paper baking cups.

2. Combine 2 cups flour, granulated sugar, brown sugar, baking powder, salt and baking soda in medium bowl. Beat milk, eggs, shortening and vanilla in large bowl with electric mixer at medium speed until well blended. Add flour mixture; beat at high speed 3 minutes, scraping side of bowl frequently.

3. Toss chocolate chips with remaining 1 tablespoon flour in small bowl; stir into batter. Spoon batter evenly into prepared muffin cups. Bake 20 minutes or until toothpick inserted into centers comes out clean. Cool cupcakes in pans on wire racks 5 minutes. Remove from pans to racks; cool completely. Decorate with frosting and candies to resemble baseballs, basketballs, soccer balls, etc. *Makes 24 cupcakes*

Banana Fudge Layer Cake

1 package DUNCAN HINES® Moist Deluxe® Classic Yellow Cake Mix
1⅓ cups water
3 eggs
⅓ cup vegetable oil
1 cup mashed ripe bananas (about 3 medium)
1 container DUNCAN HINES® Creamy Home-Style Classic Chocolate
Frosting

1. Preheat oven to 350°F. Grease and flour two 9-inch round cake pans.

2. Combine cake mix, water, eggs and oil in large bowl. Beat at low speed with electric mixer until moistened. Beat at medium speed 2 minutes. Stir in bananas. Pour into prepared pans. Bake at 350°F for 28 to 31 minutes or until toothpick inserted into centers comes out clean. Cool in pans 15 minutes. Remove from pans; cool completely.

3. Fill and frost cake with frosting. Garnish as desired.

Makes 12 to 16 servings

Cookie Pizza Cake

1 package (16 ounces) refrigerated chocolate chip cookie dough
1 package (about 18 ounces) chocolate cake mix, plus ingredients to prepare mix
1 cup prepared vanilla frosting
½ cup peanut butter
1 to 2 tablespoons milk
1 container (16 ounces) chocolate frosting
Chocolate peanut butter cups, chopped (optional)
Peanut butter chips (optional)

1. Preheat oven to 350°F. Spray two 12-inch pizza pans with nonstick cooking spray. Press cookie dough evenly into one pan. Bake 15 to 20 minutes or until edges are golden brown. Cool in pan on wire rack 20 minutes. Remove from pan to wire rack; cool completely.

2. Prepare cake mix according to package directions. Fill second pan one-fourth to half full with batter. (Reserve remaining cake batter for another use, such as cupcakes.) Bake 10 to 15 minutes or until toothpick inserted into center comes out clean. Cool in pan on wire rack 15 minutes. Gently remove cake from pan; cool completely on rack. Combine vanilla frosting and peanut butter in small bowl. Gradually stir in milk, 1 tablespoon at a time, until mixture is of spreadable consistency.

3. Place cookie on serving plate. Spread peanut butter frosting over cookie. Place cake on top of cookie, trimming cookie to match the size of cake, if necessary. Frost top and side of cake with chocolate frosting. Garnish with peanut butter cups and peanut butter chips.

Makes 12 to 14 servings

Chocolate Peanut Butter Cookies

1 package DUNCAN HINES® Moist Deluxe® Devil's Food Cake Mix
¾ cup crunchy peanut butter
2 eggs
2 tablespoons milk
1 cup candy-coated peanut butter pieces*

You may substitute 1 cup peanut butter chips in place of peanut butter pieces.

1. Preheat oven to 350°F. Grease baking sheets.

2. Combine cake mix, peanut butter, eggs and milk in large mixing bowl. Beat at low speed with electric mixer until blended. Stir in peanut butter pieces.

3. Drop dough by slightly rounded tablespoonfuls onto prepared baking sheets. Bake 7 to 9 minutes or until lightly browned. Cool 2 minutes on baking sheets. Remove to cooling racks. Cool completely. Store in airtight container.

Makes about 3½ dozen cookies

Lazy Daisy Cupcakes

**1 package (about 18 ounces)
yellow cake mix, plus
ingredients to prepare mix
Yellow food coloring
1 container (16 ounces) vanilla
frosting
30 large marshmallows
24 small round candies or
gumdrops**

1. Preheat oven to 350°F. Line 24 standard (2½-inch) muffin cups with paper baking cups or spray with nonstick cooking spray. Prepare cake mix and bake in prepared muffin cups according to package directions. Cool cupcakes in pans on wire racks 15 minutes. Remove from pans to racks; cool completely.

2. Add food coloring to frosting in small bowl, a few drops at a time, until desired shade of yellow is reached. Frost cupcakes.

3. Cut each marshmallow crosswise into 4 pieces with scissors. Stretch pieces into petal shapes; place 5 pieces on each cupcake to form flower. Place round candy in center of each flower. *Makes 24 cupcakes*

S'More Bars

1 package (16 ounces) refrigerated chocolate chip cookie dough
¼ cup graham cracker crumbs
3 cups mini marshmallows
½ cup semisweet or milk chocolate chips
2 teaspoons shortening

1. Preheat oven to 350°F. Grease 13×9-inch baking pan. Press dough into prepared pan. Sprinkle evenly with graham cracker crumbs.

2. Bake 10 to 12 minutes or until edges are golden brown. Sprinkle with marshmallows. Bake 2 to 3 minutes or until marshmallows are puffed. Cool completely in pan on wire rack.

3. Combine chocolate chips and shortening in small resealable food storage bag; seal. Microwave on HIGH 1 minute; knead bag lightly. Microwave on HIGH for additional 30-second intervals or until chips and shortening are completely melted and smooth, kneading bag after each 30-second interval. Cut off small corner of bag. Drizzle chocolate mixture over bars. Refrigerate 5 to 10 minutes or until chocolate is set. Cut into bars.   *Makes 3 dozen bars*

Acknowledgments

The publisher would like to thank the companies and organizations listed below for the use of their recipes and photographs in this publication.

Cherry Marketing Institute

Del Monte Foods

Duncan Hines® and Moist Deluxe® are registered trademarks of Pinnacle Foods Corp.

The Golden Grain Company®

The Hershey Company

®, ™, © 2009 Kellogg NA Co.

Nestlé USA

Reckitt Benckiser Inc.

Sargento® Foods Inc.

Unilever

METRIC CONVERSION CHART

VOLUME MEASUREMENTS (dry)

1/8 teaspoon = 0.5 mL
1/4 teaspoon = 1 mL
1/2 teaspoon = 2 mL
3/4 teaspoon = 4 mL
1 teaspoon = 5 mL
1 tablespoon = 15 mL
2 tablespoons = 30 mL
1/4 cup = 60 mL
1/3 cup = 75 mL
1/2 cup = 125 mL
2/3 cup = 150 mL
3/4 cup = 175 mL
1 cup = 250 mL
2 cups = 1 pint = 500 mL
3 cups = 750 mL
4 cups = 1 quart = 1 L

VOLUME MEASUREMENTS (fluid)

1 fluid ounce (2 tablespoons) = 30 mL
4 fluid ounces (1/2 cup) = 125 mL
8 fluid ounces (1 cup) = 250 mL
12 fluid ounces (1 1/2 cups) = 375 mL
16 fluid ounces (2 cups) = 500 mL

WEIGHTS (mass)

1/2 ounce = 15 g
1 ounce = 30 g
3 ounces = 90 g
4 ounces = 120 g
8 ounces = 225 g
10 ounces = 285 g
12 ounces = 360 g
16 ounces = 1 pound = 450 g

DIMENSIONS

1/16 inch = 2 mm
1/8 inch = 3 mm
1/4 inch = 6 mm
1/2 inch = 1.5 cm
3/4 inch = 2 cm
1 inch = 2.5 cm

OVEN TEMPERATURES

250°F = 120°C
275°F = 140°C
300°F = 150°C
325°F = 160°C
350°F = 180°C
375°F = 190°C
400°F = 200°C
425°F = 220°C
450°F = 230°C

BAKING PAN SIZES

Utensil	Size in Inches/Quarts	Metric Volume	Size in Centimeters
Baking or Cake Pan (square or rectangular)	8×8×2	2 L	20×20×5
	9×9×2	2.5 L	23×23×5
	12×8×2	3 L	30×20×5
	13×9×2	3.5 L	33×23×5
Loaf Pan	8×4×3	1.5 L	20×10×7
	9×5×3	2 L	23×13×7
Round Layer Cake Pan	8×1½	1.2 L	20×4
	9×1½	1.5 L	23×4
Pie Plate	8×1¼	750 mL	20×3
	9×1¼	1 L	23×3
Baking Dish or Casserole	1 quart	1 L	—
	1½ quart	1.5 L	—
	2 quart	2 L	—